CLICK IT

stepro books

CL1CK IT

"Photography is a way of feeling, of touching, of loving. What you have caught on film is captured forever... It remembers little things, long after you have forgotten everything."
— **Aaron Siskind**

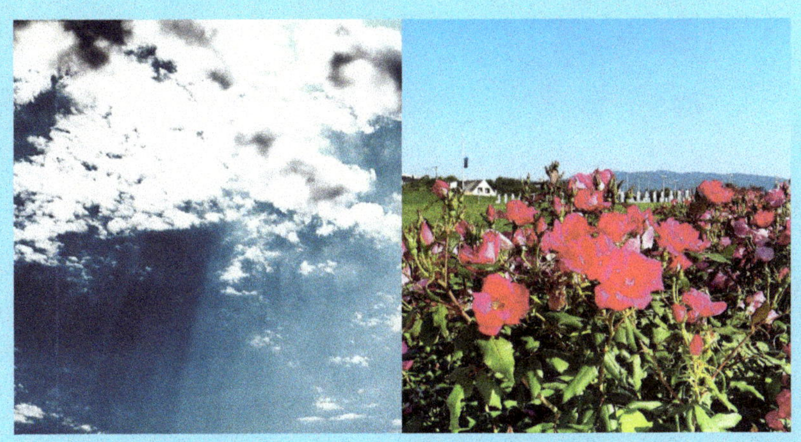

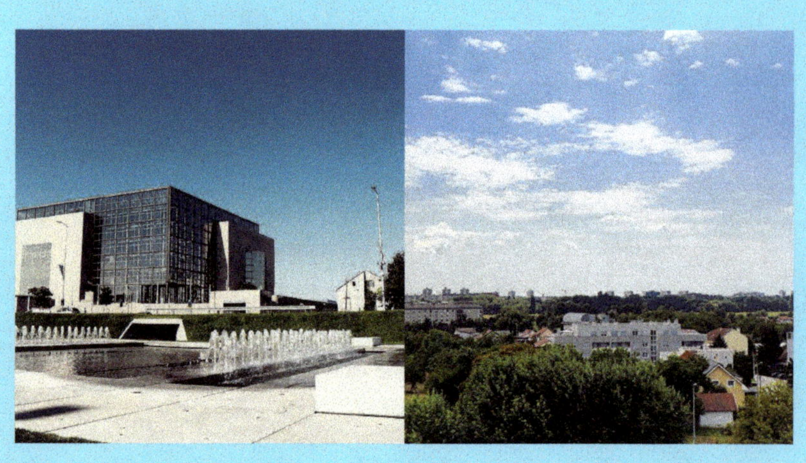

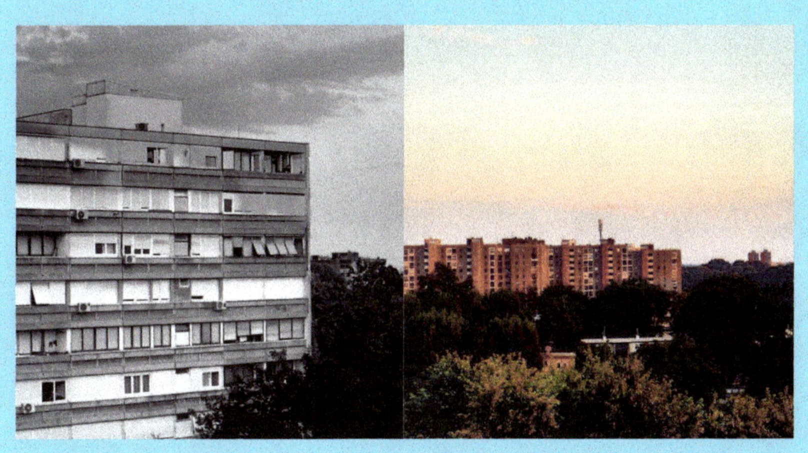

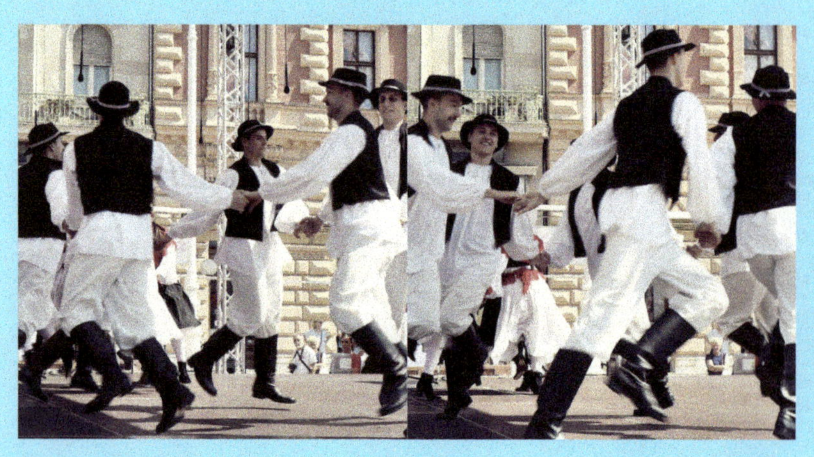

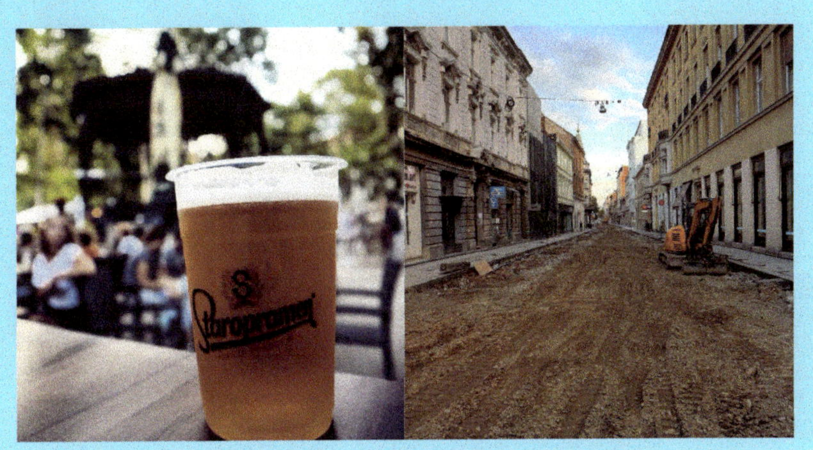

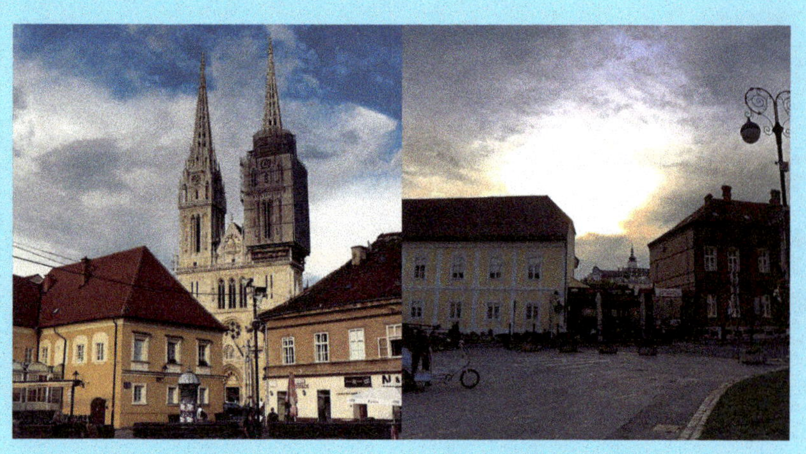

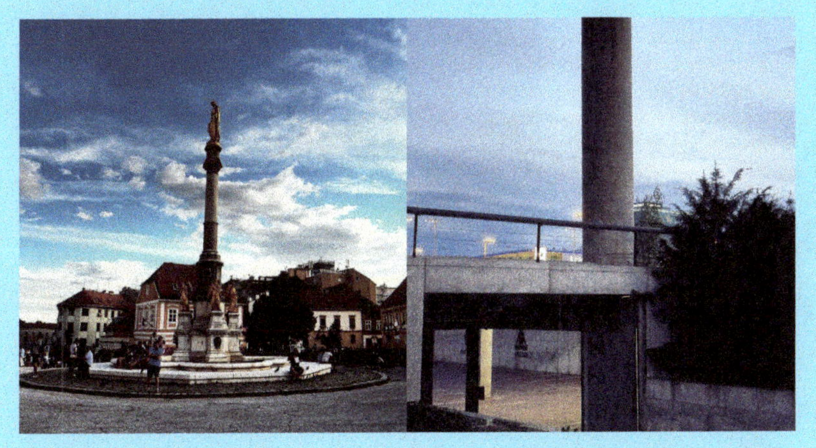

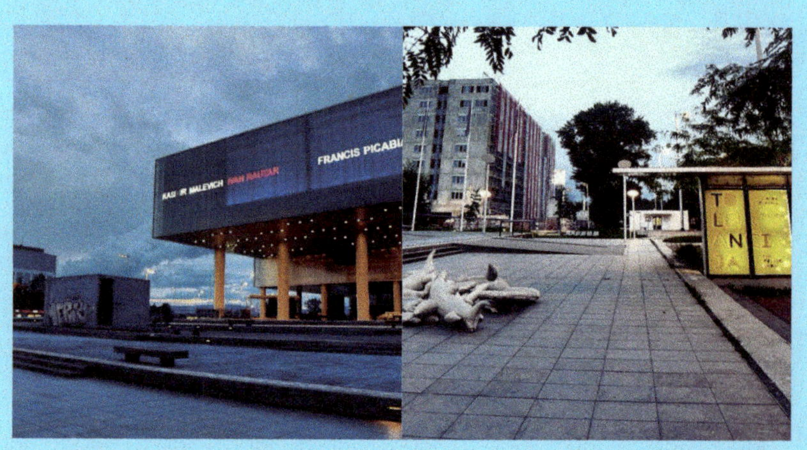
KASIMIR MALEVICH IVAN PUNI FRANCIS PICABIA
T L
N I
A

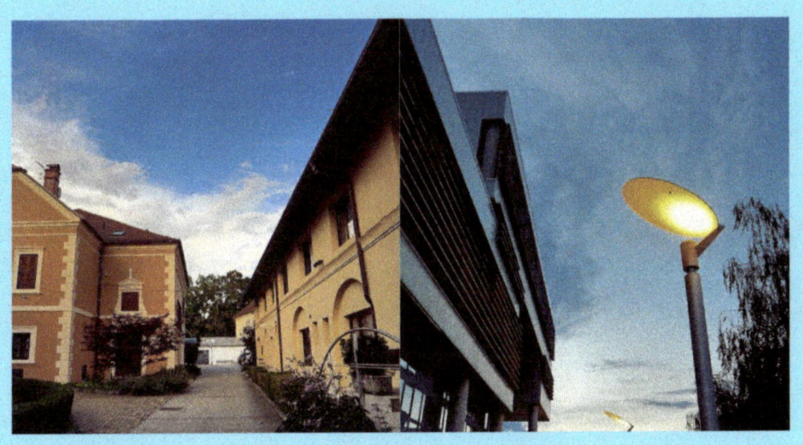

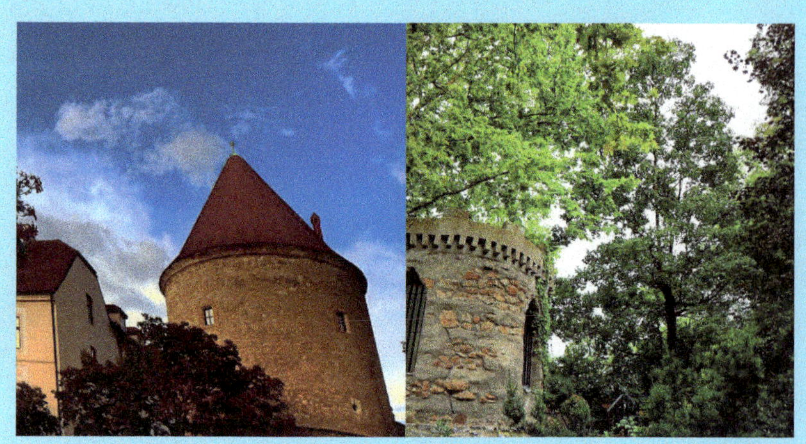

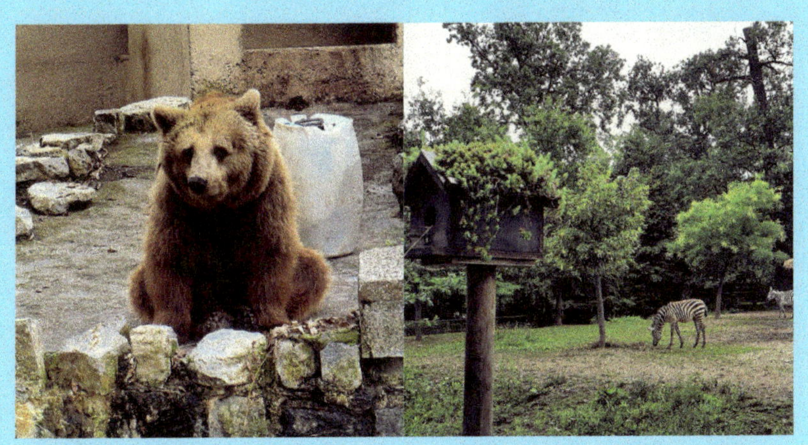

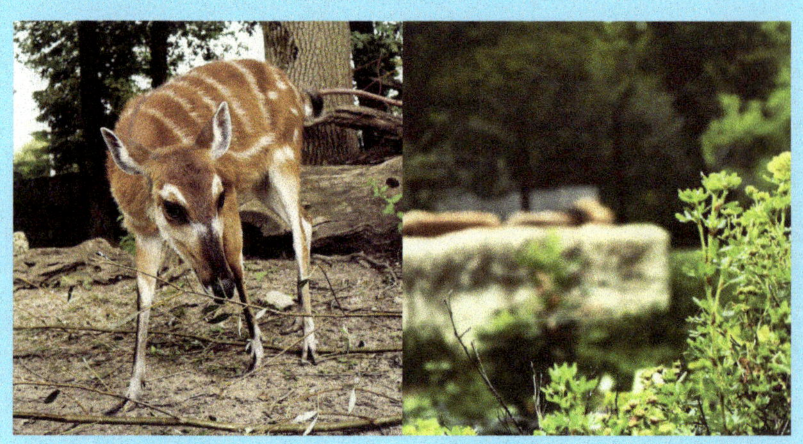

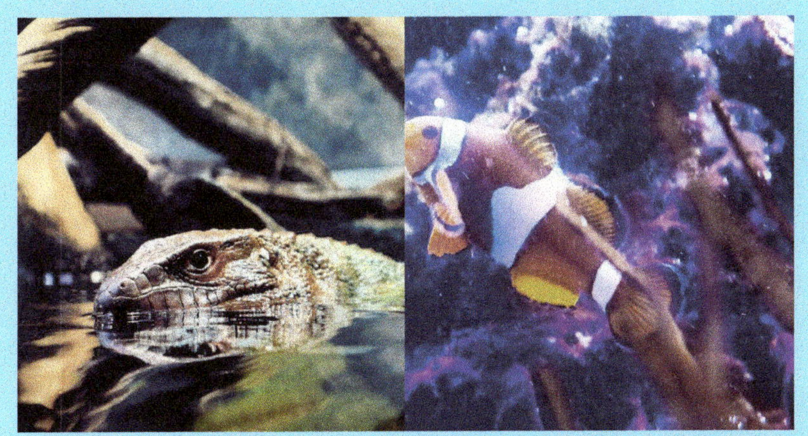

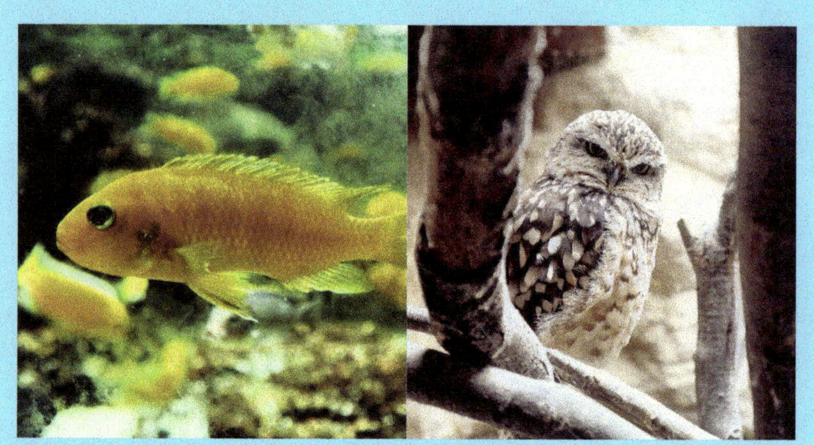

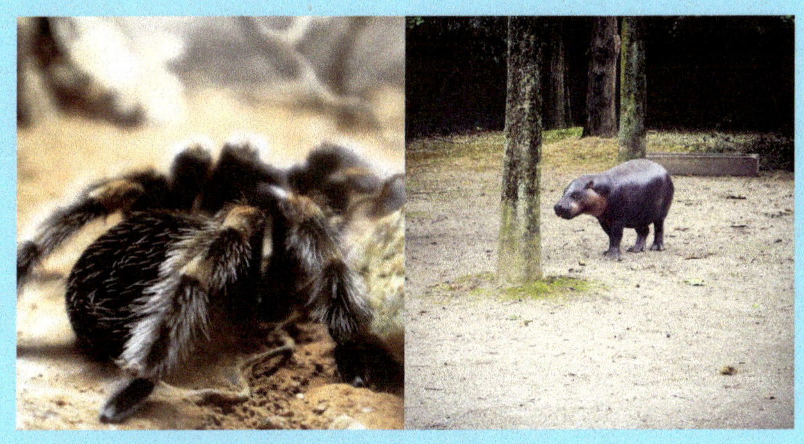

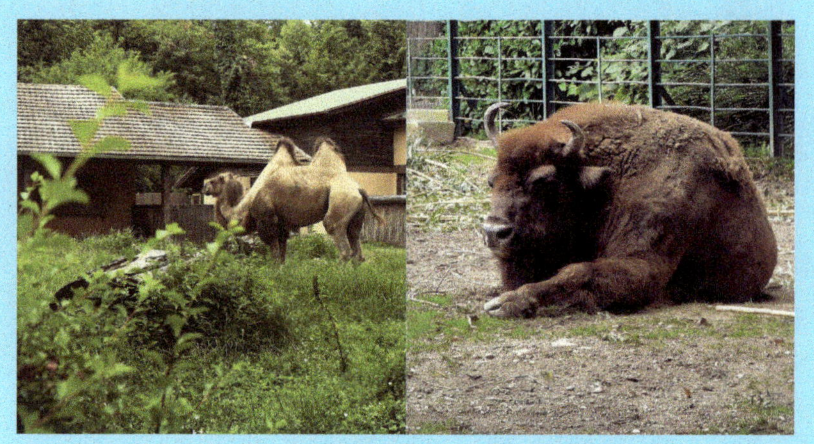

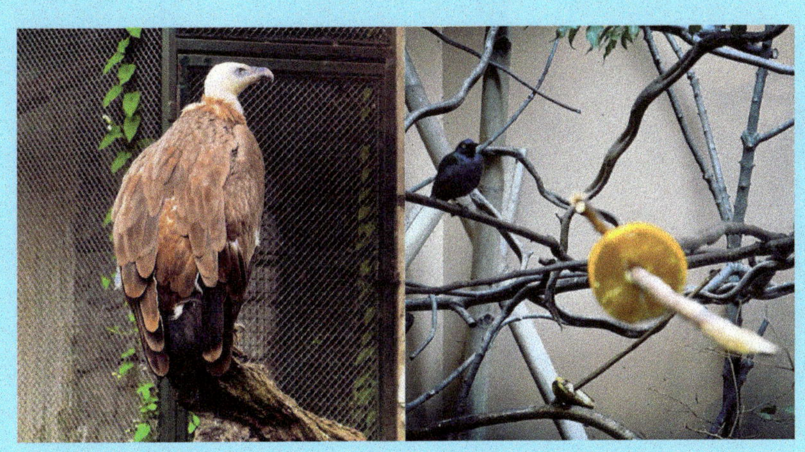

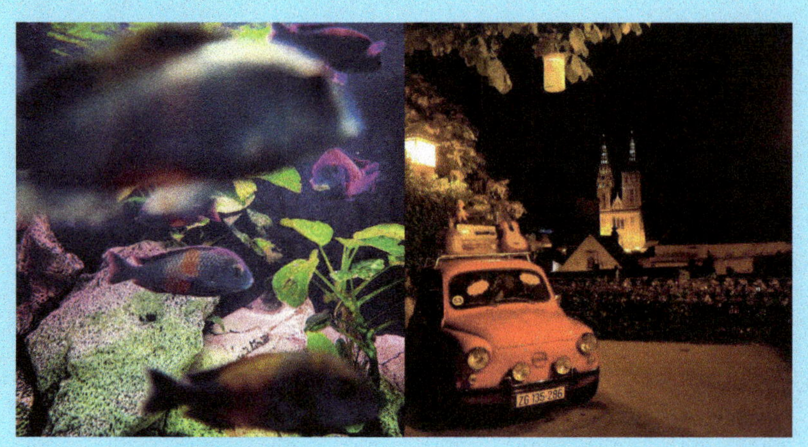

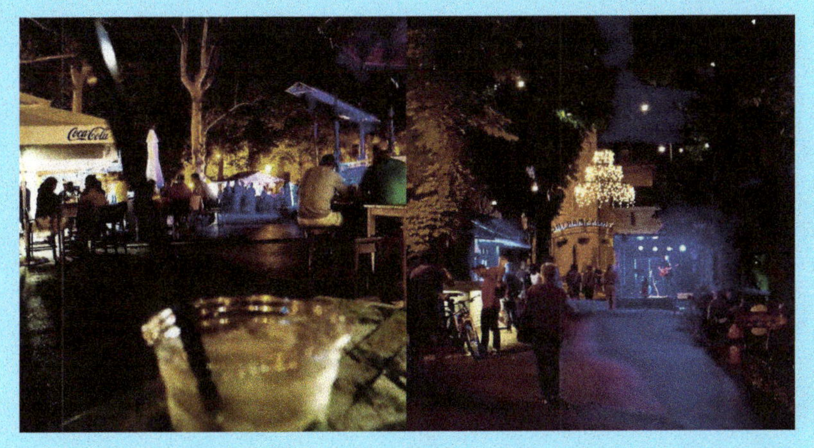

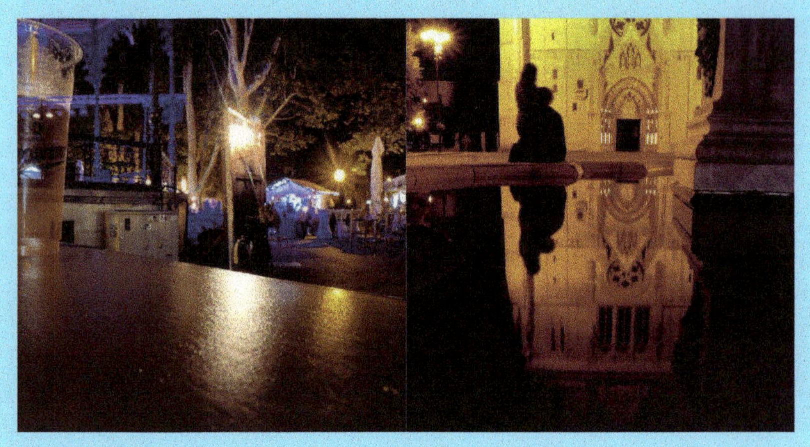

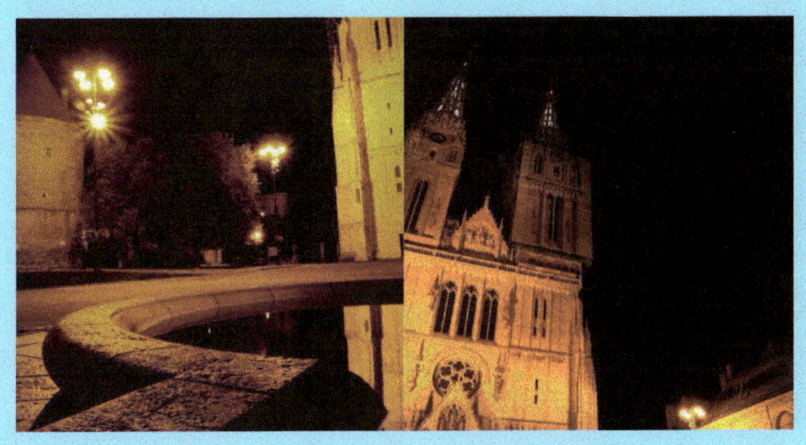

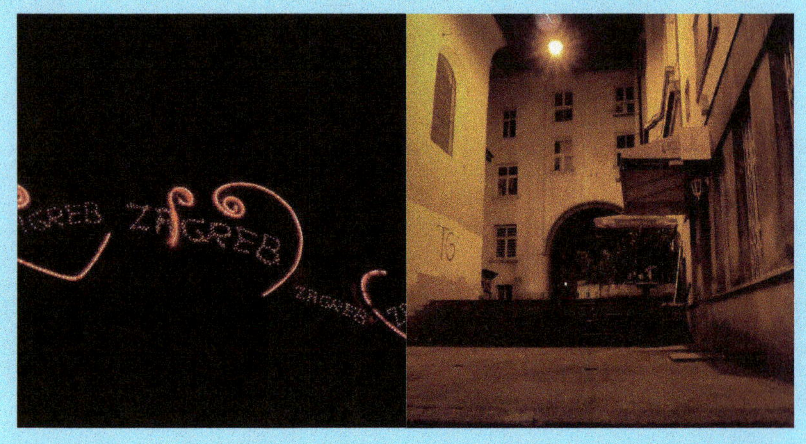

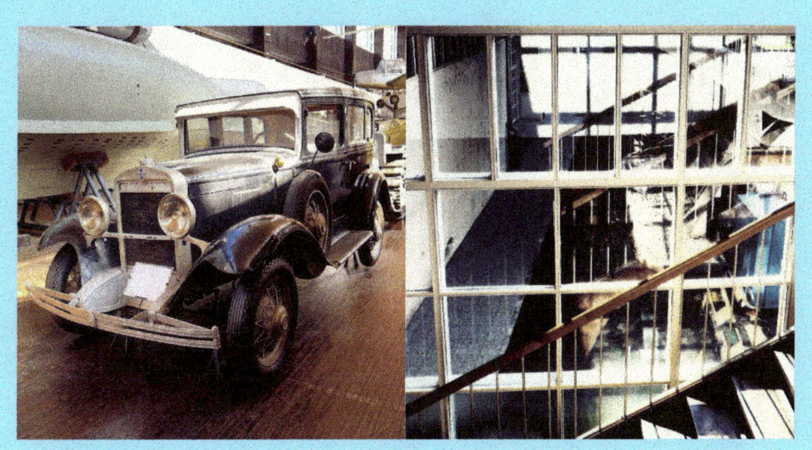

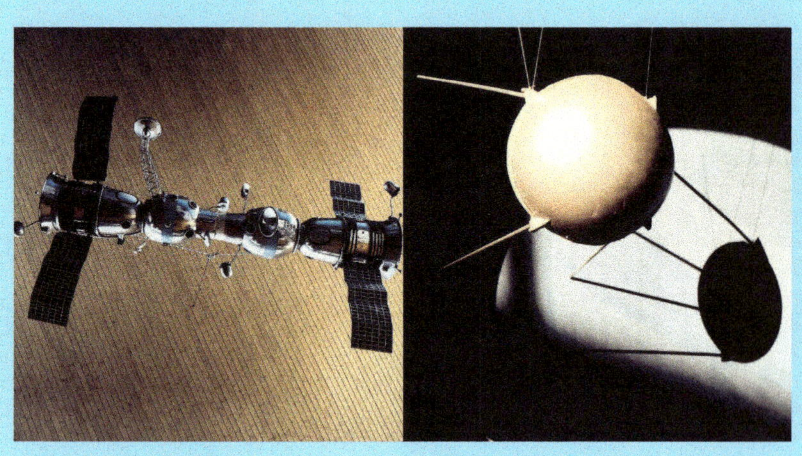

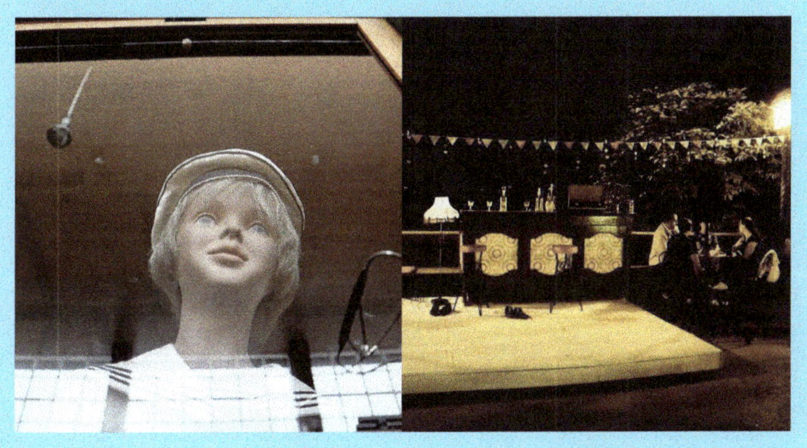

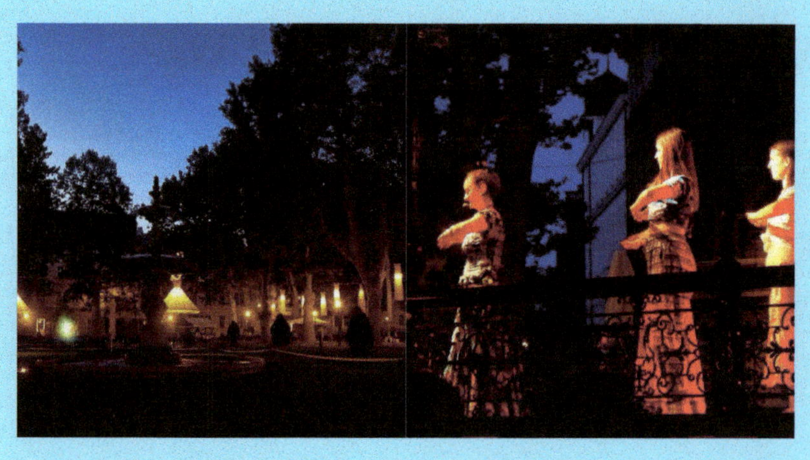

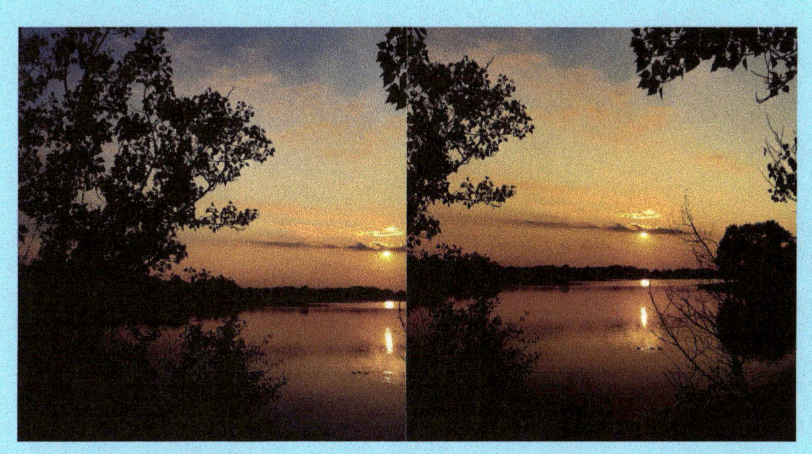

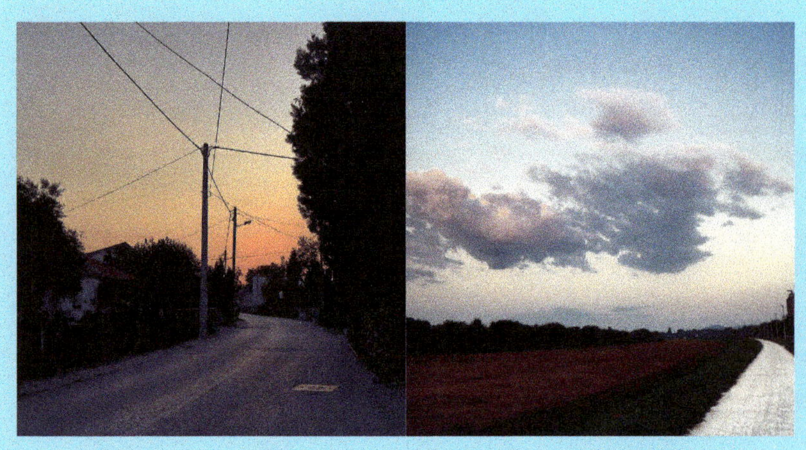

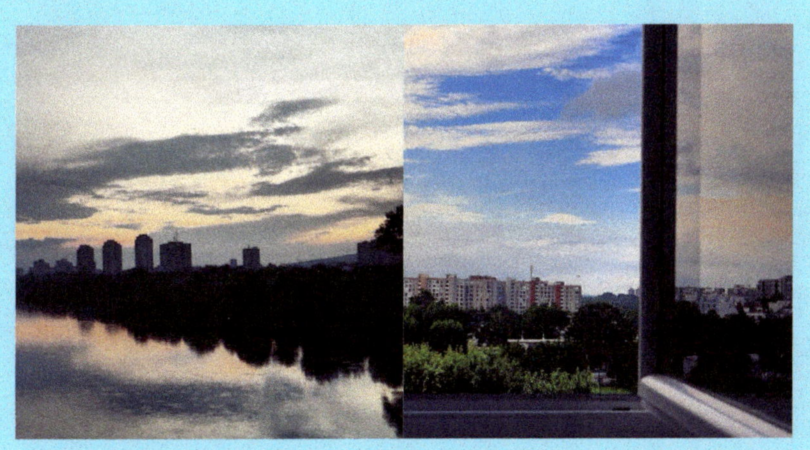

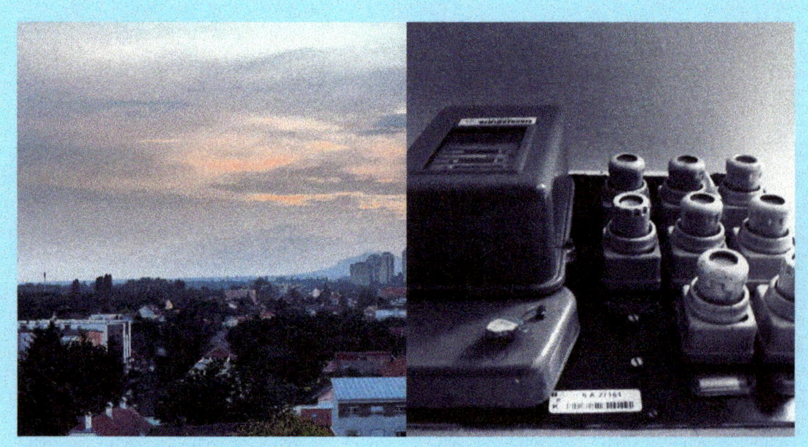

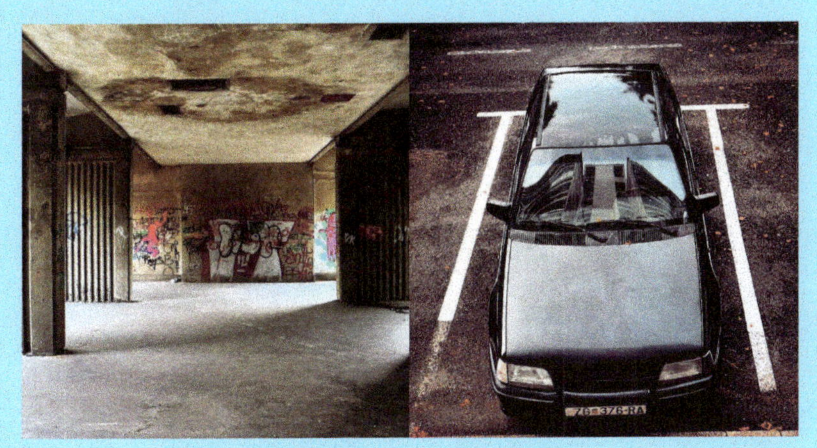

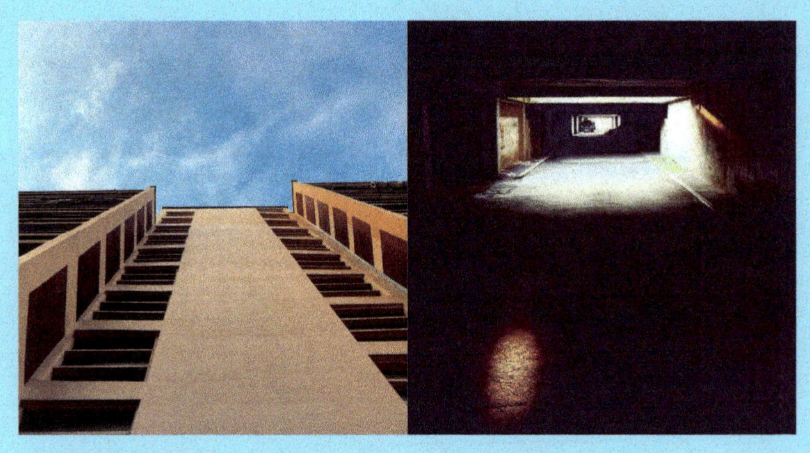

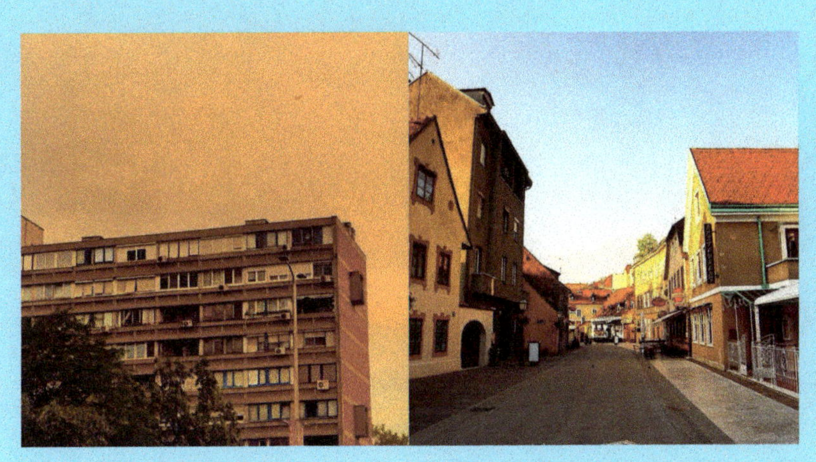

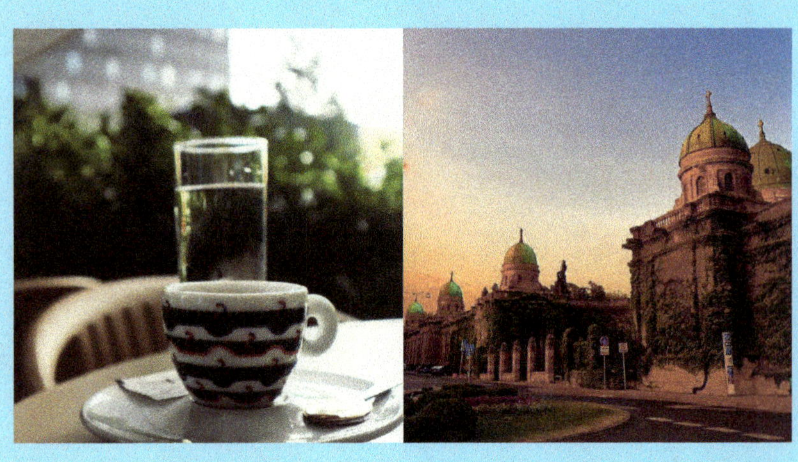

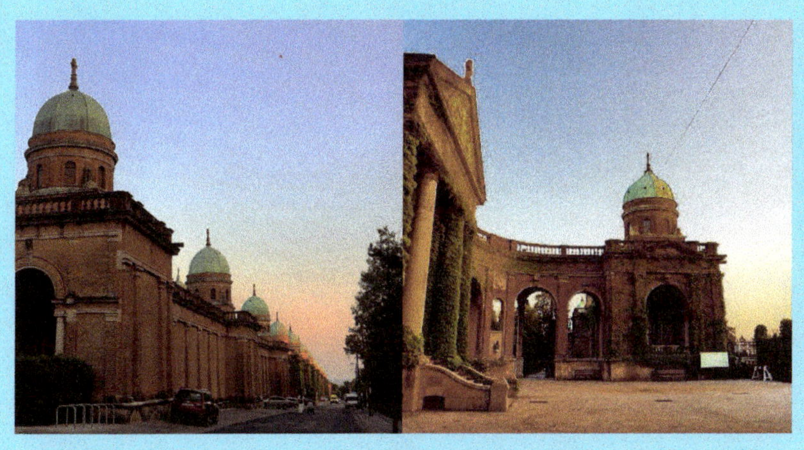

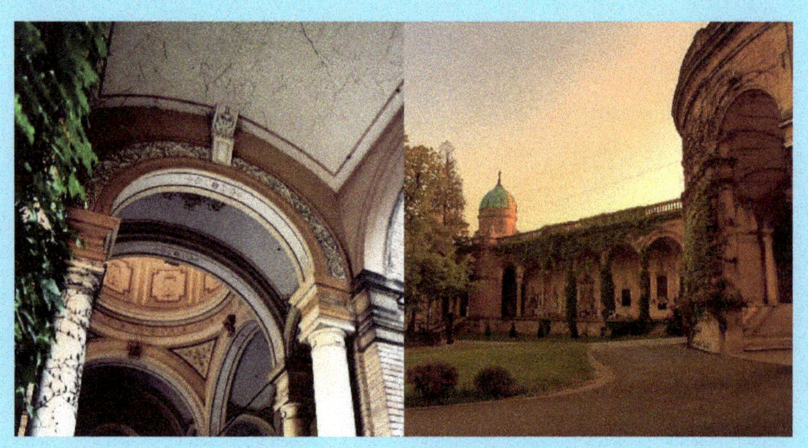

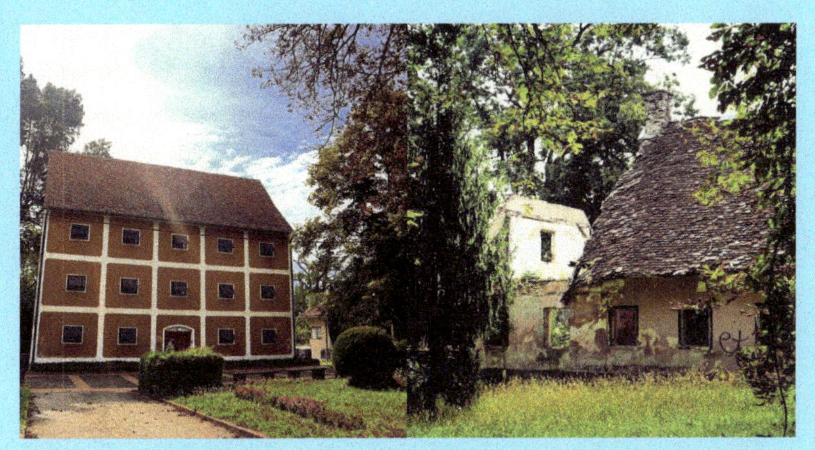

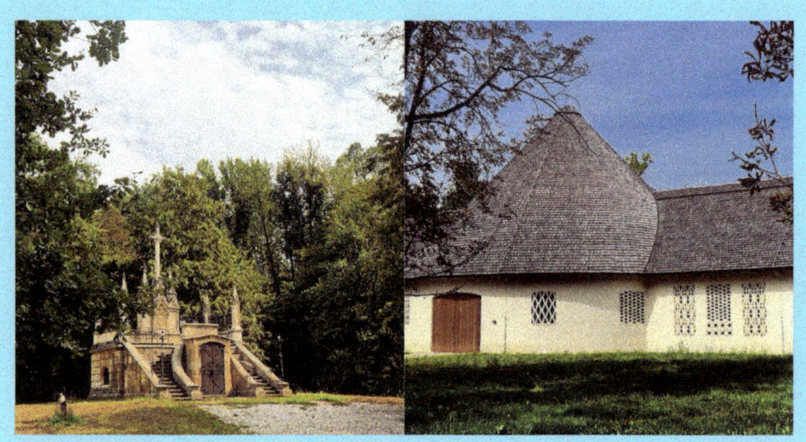

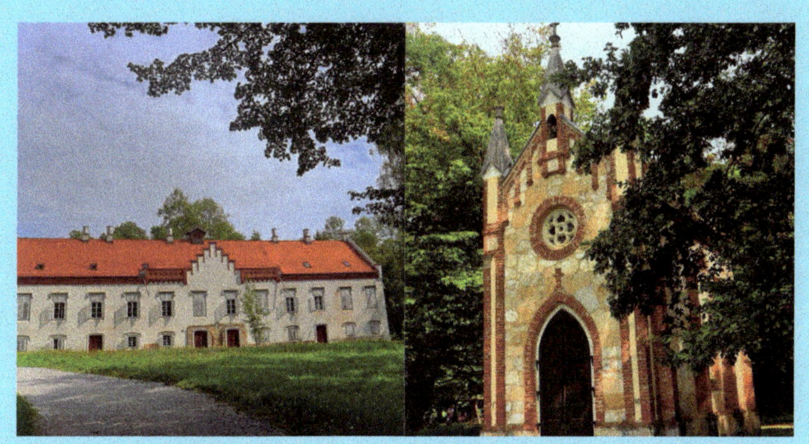

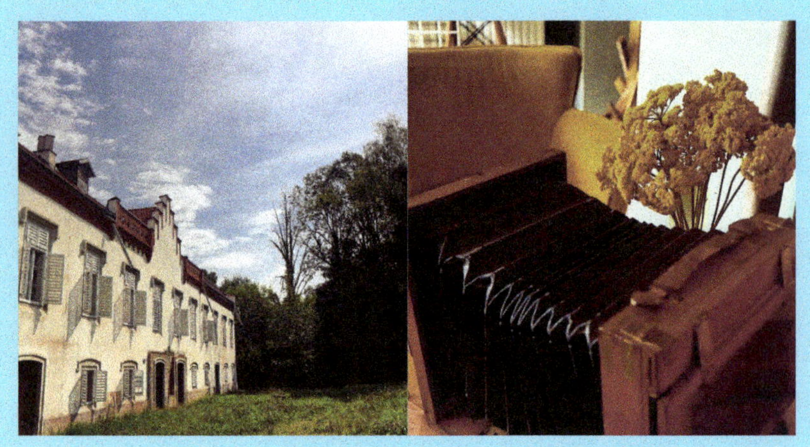

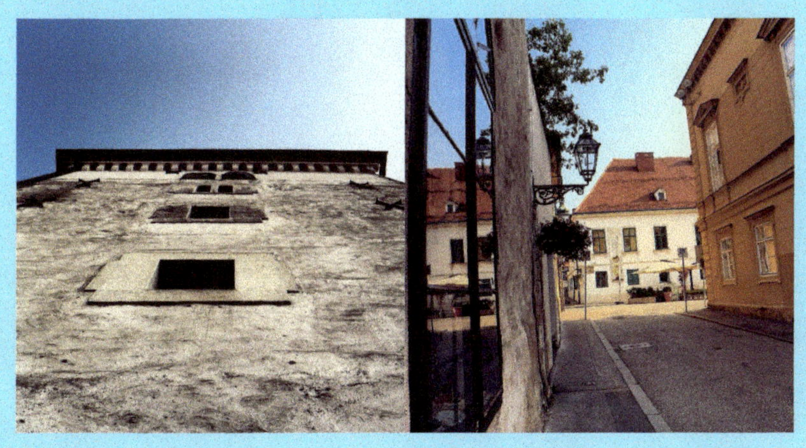

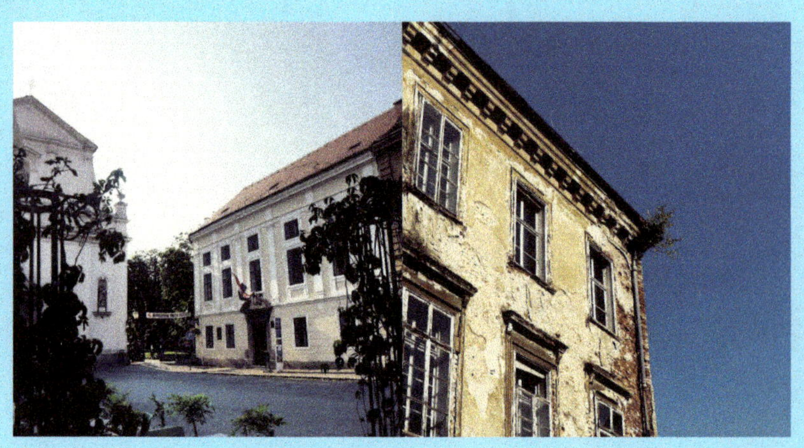

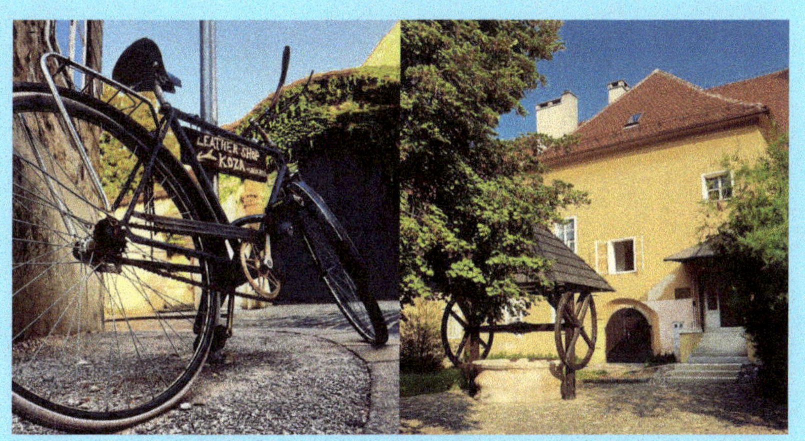

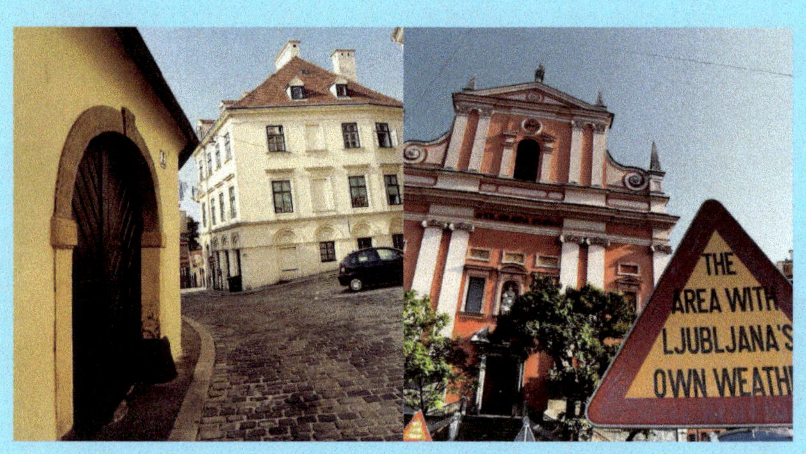

THE
AREA WITH
LJUBLJANA'S
OWN WEATH

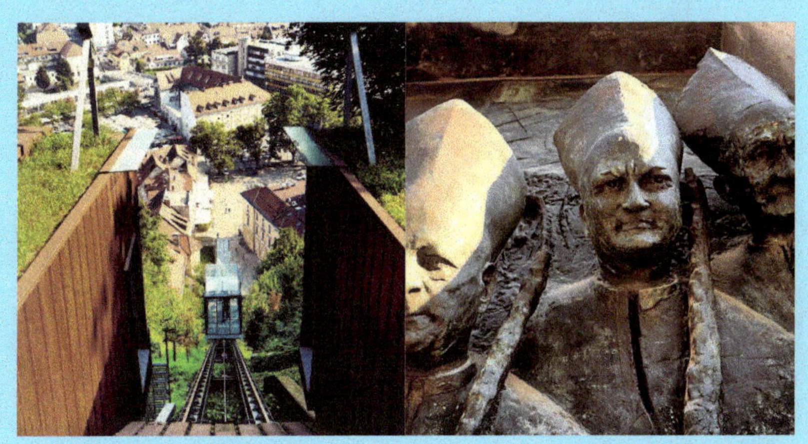

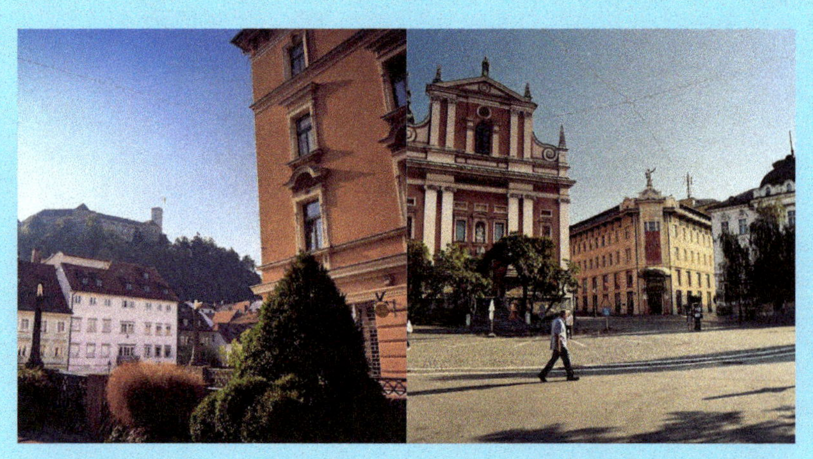

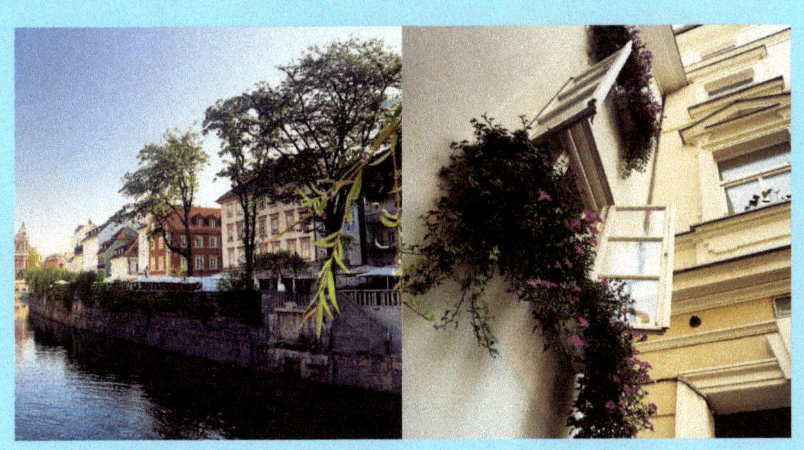

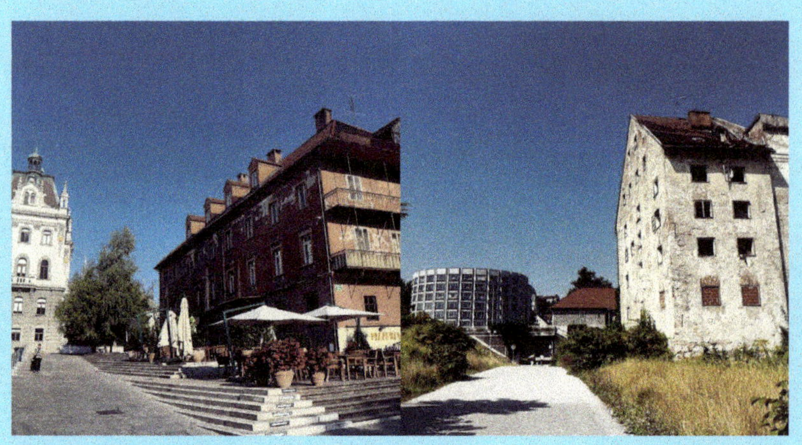

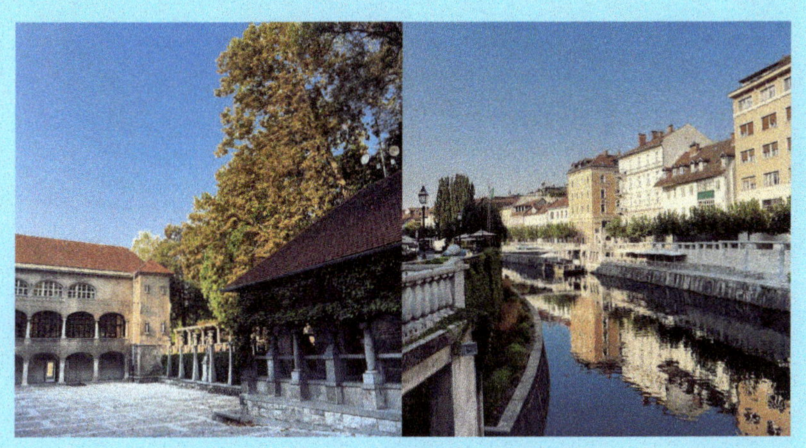

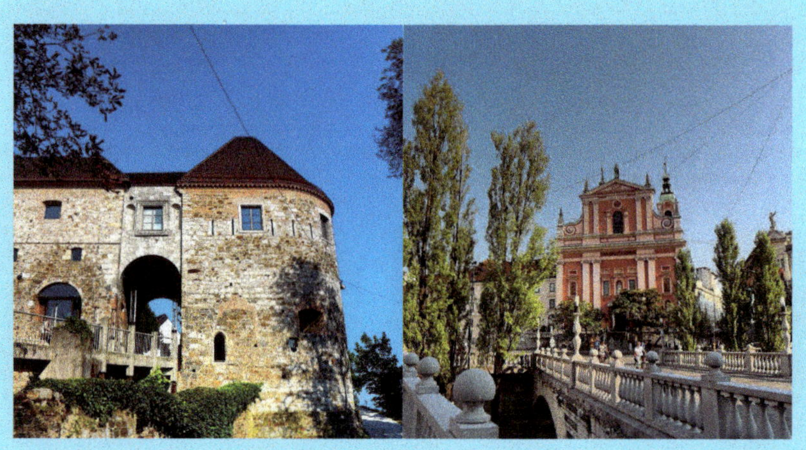

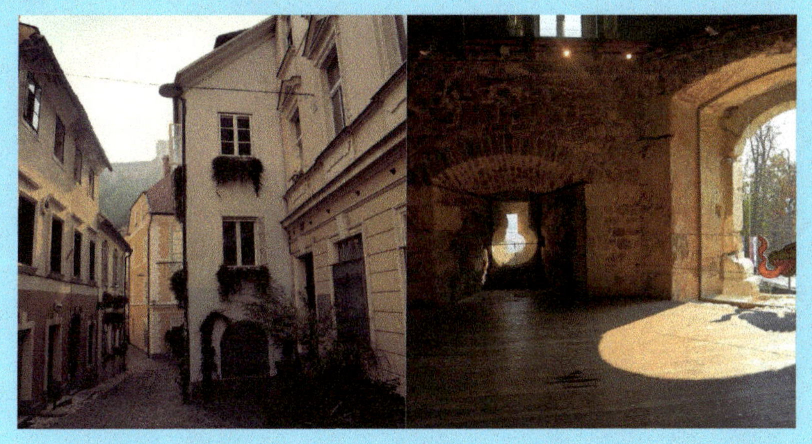

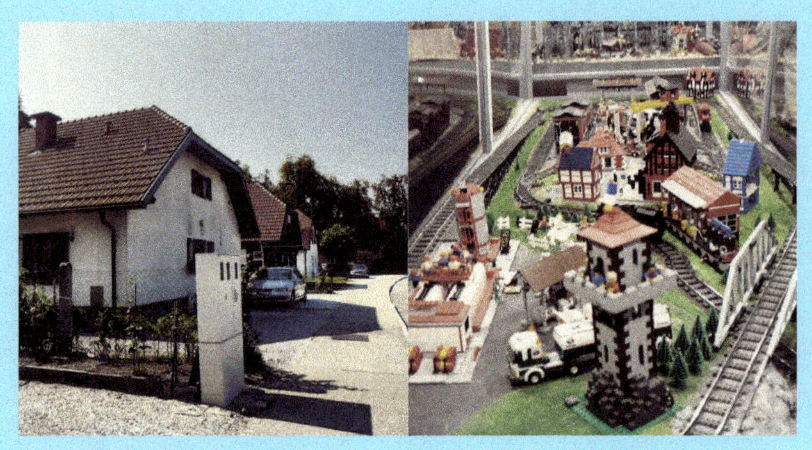

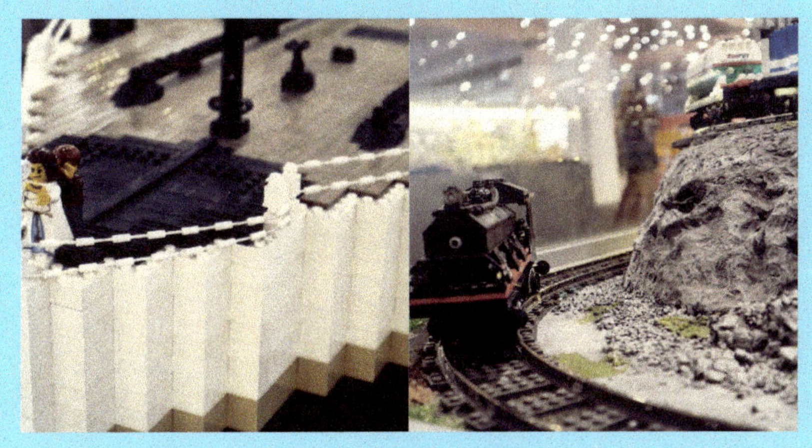

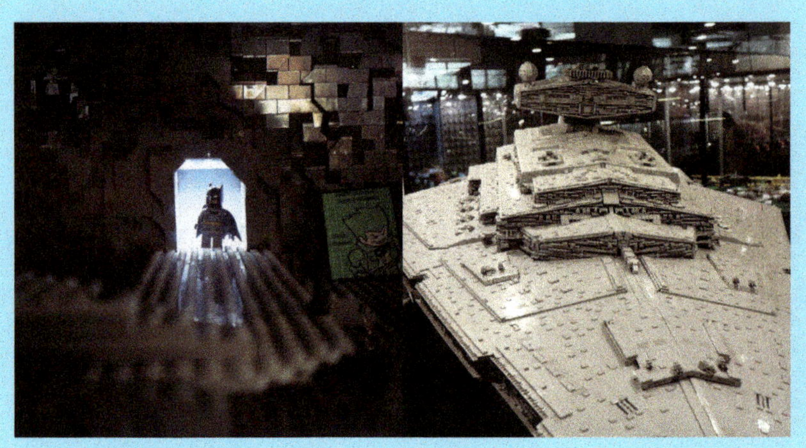

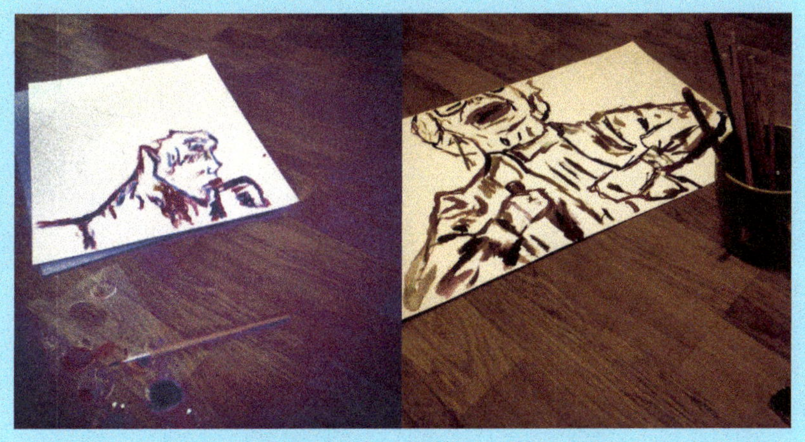

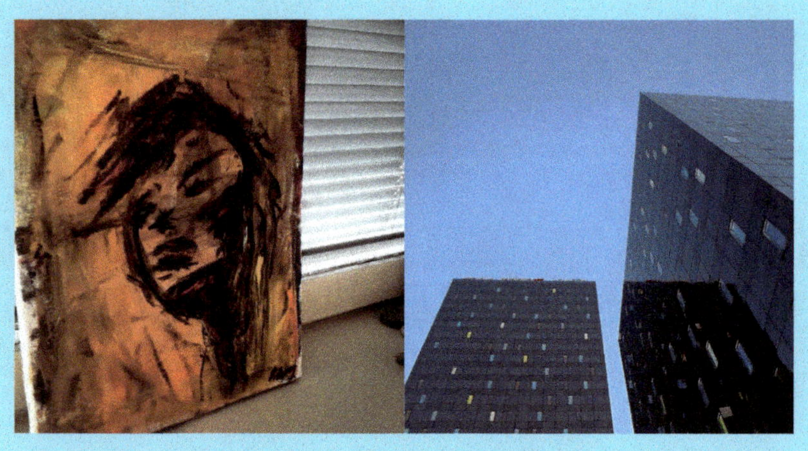

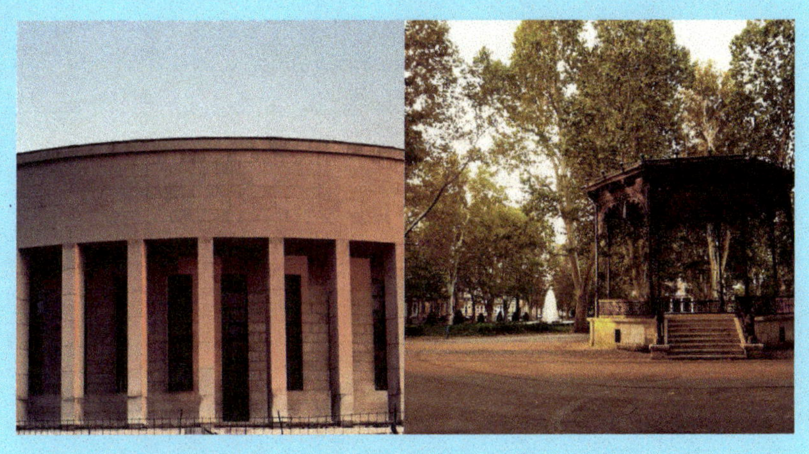

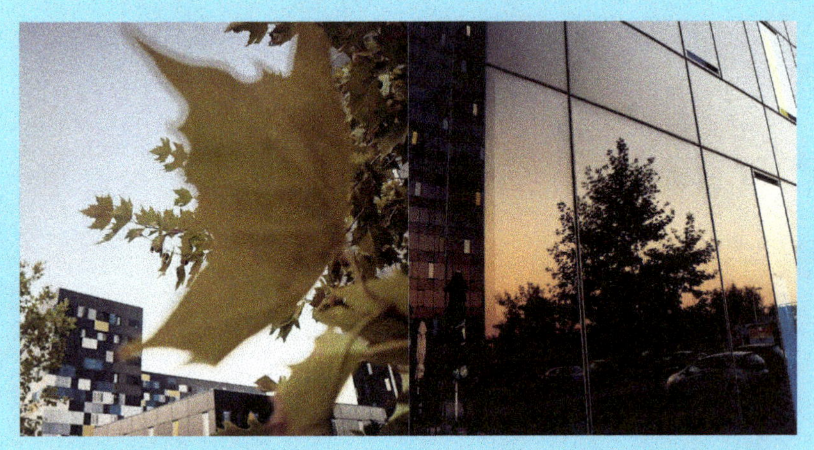

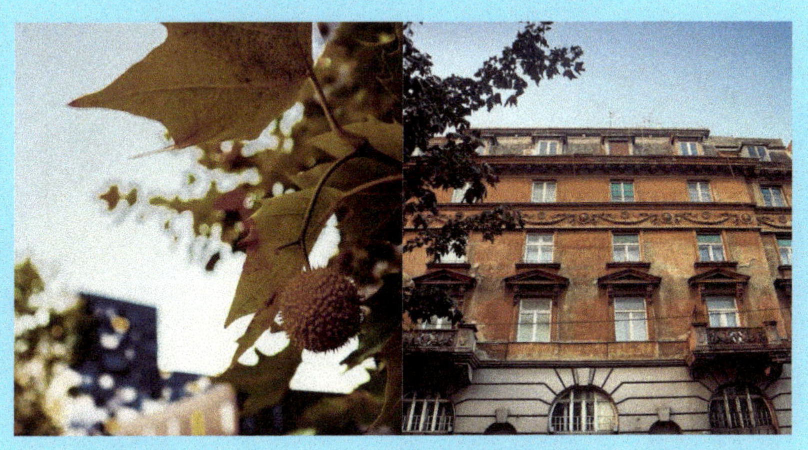

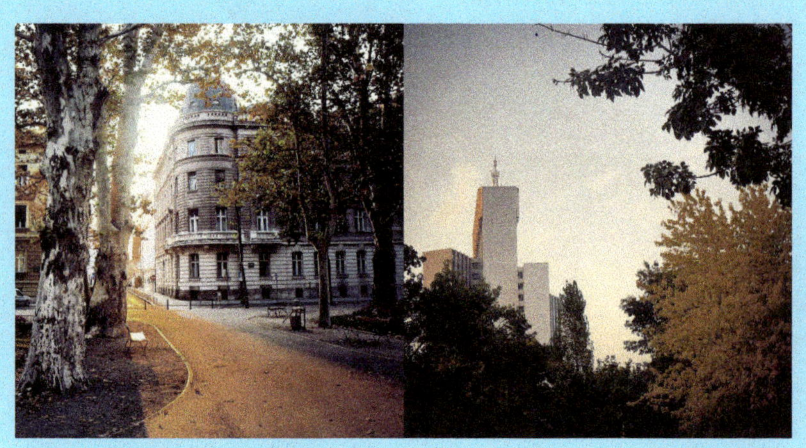

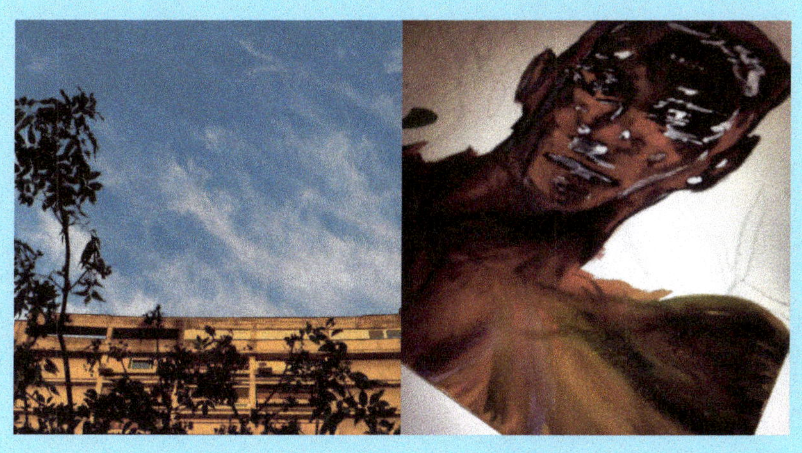

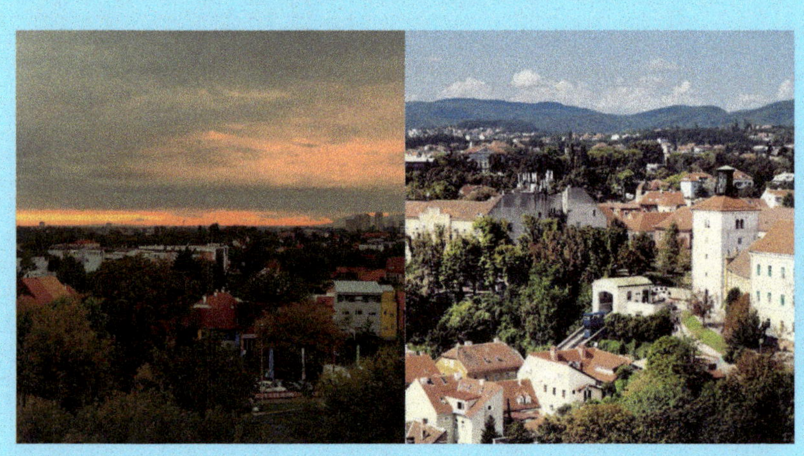

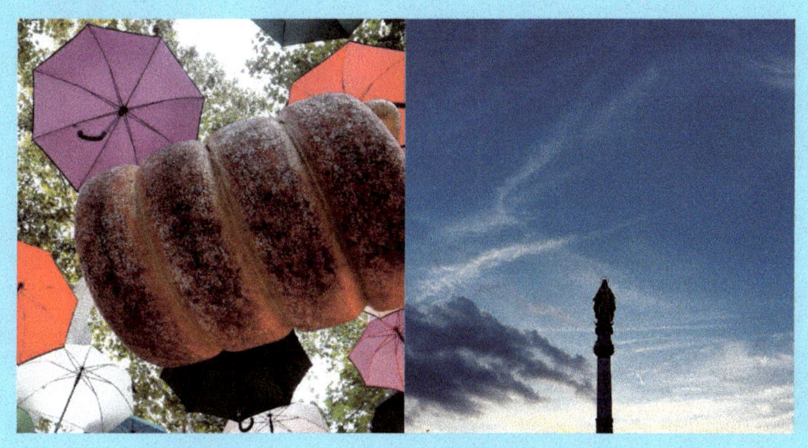

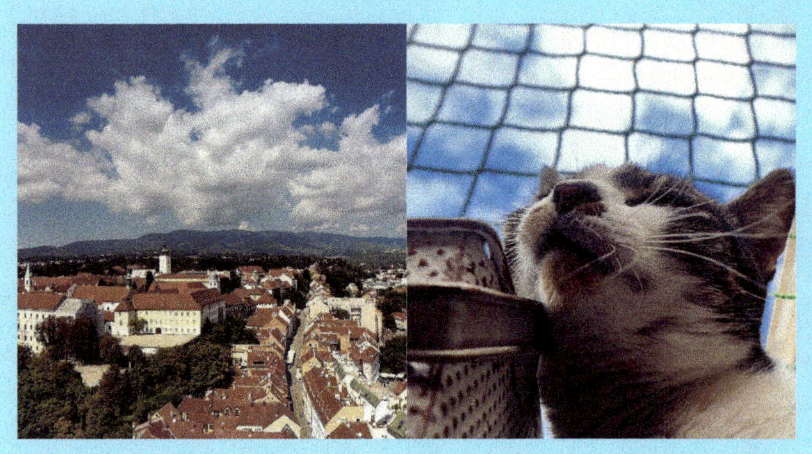

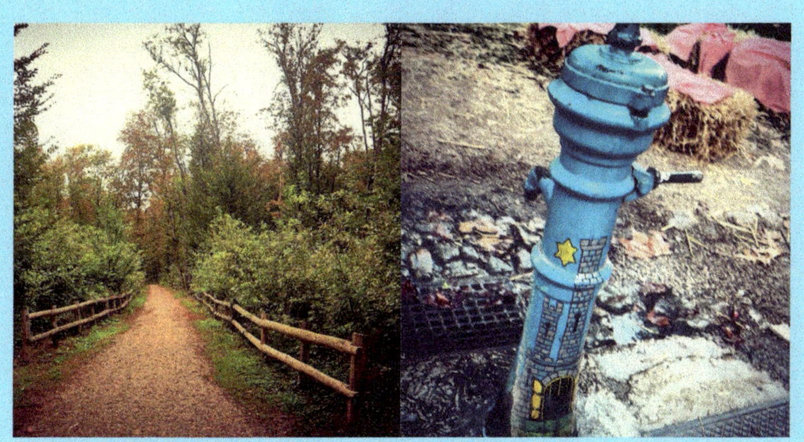

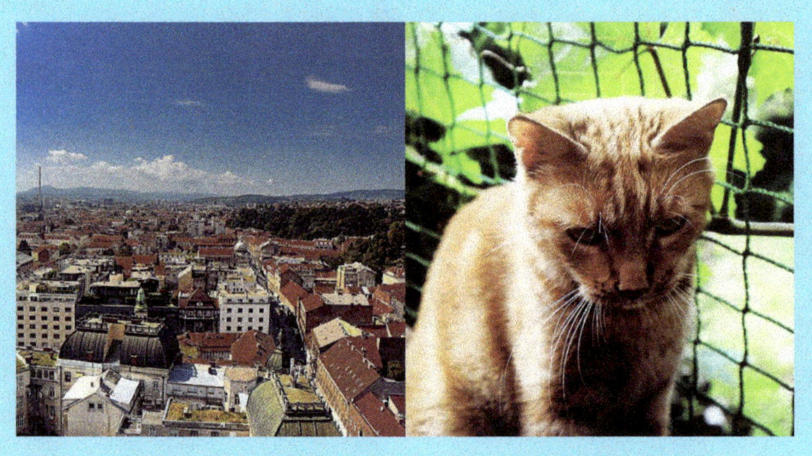

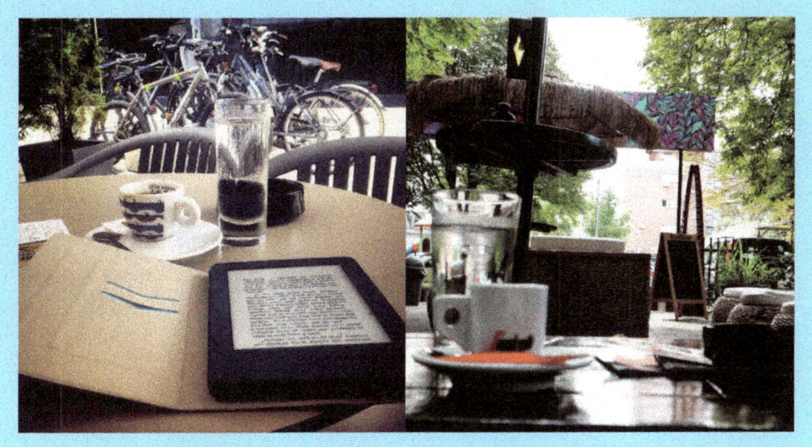

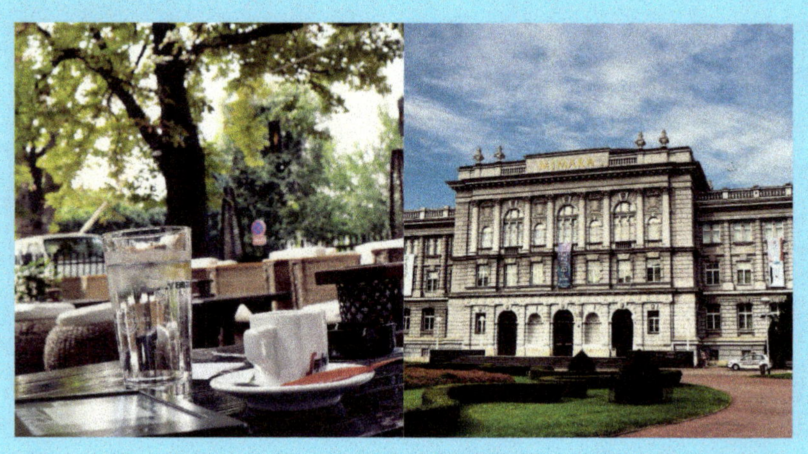

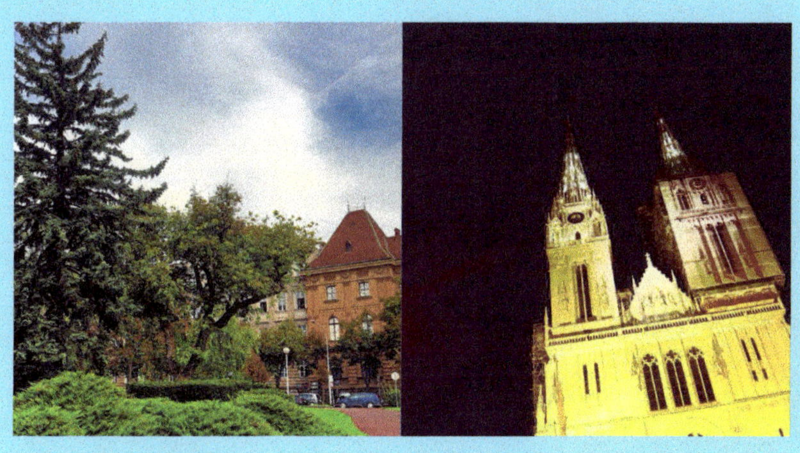

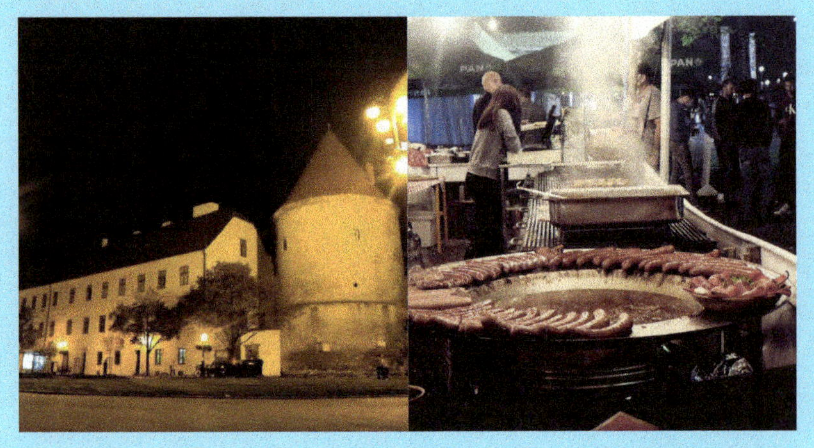

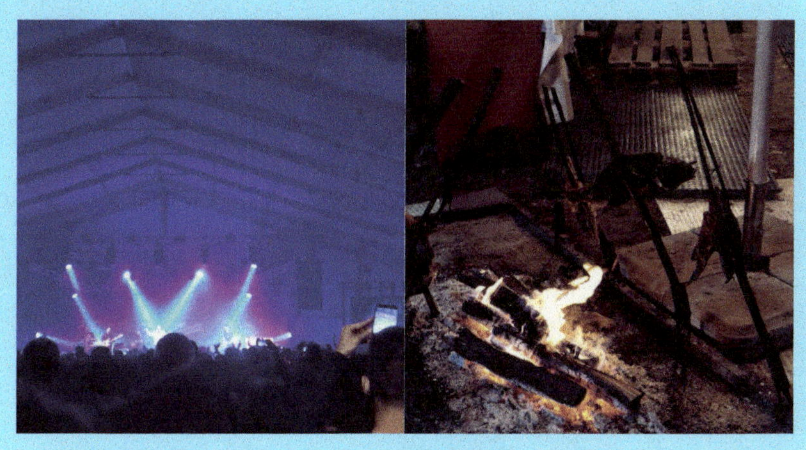

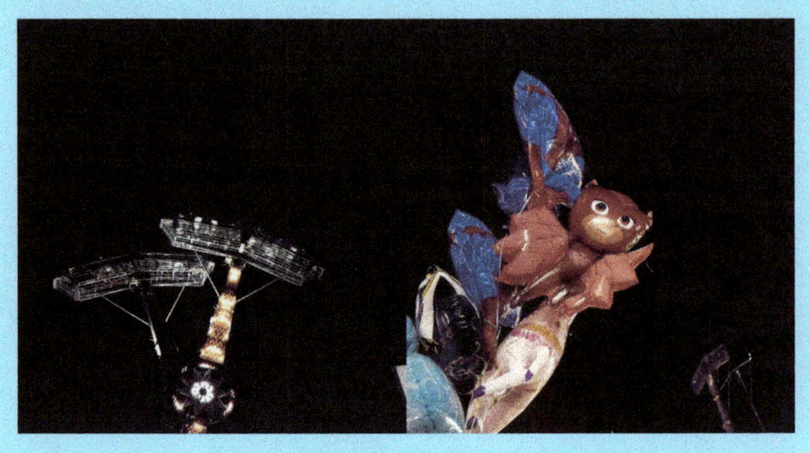

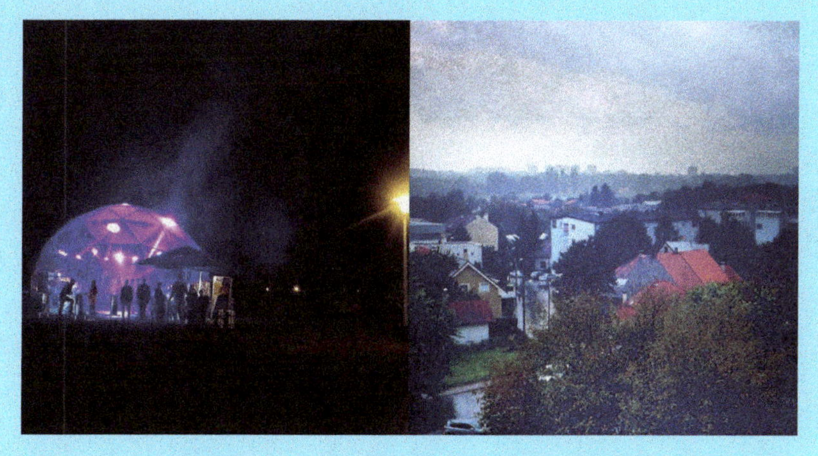

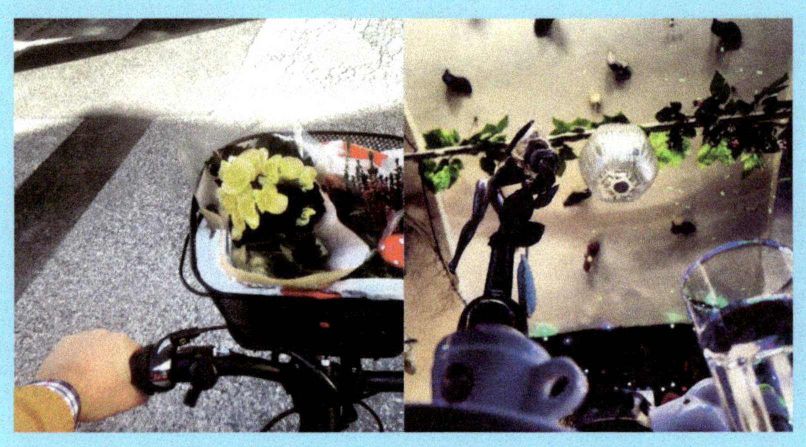

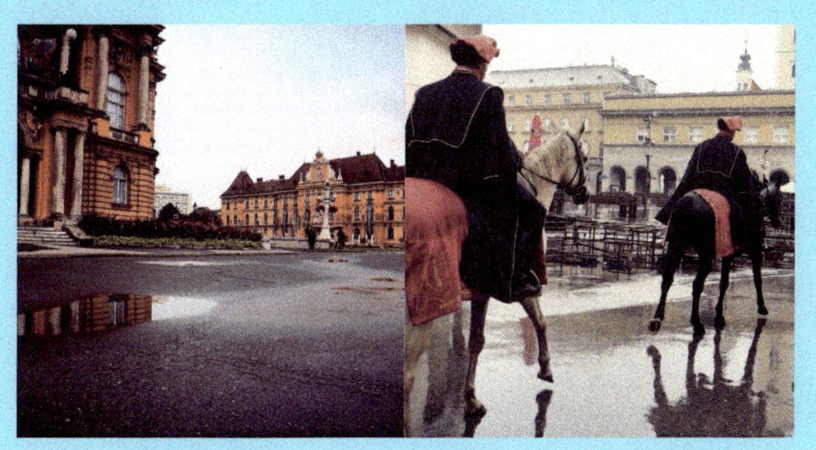

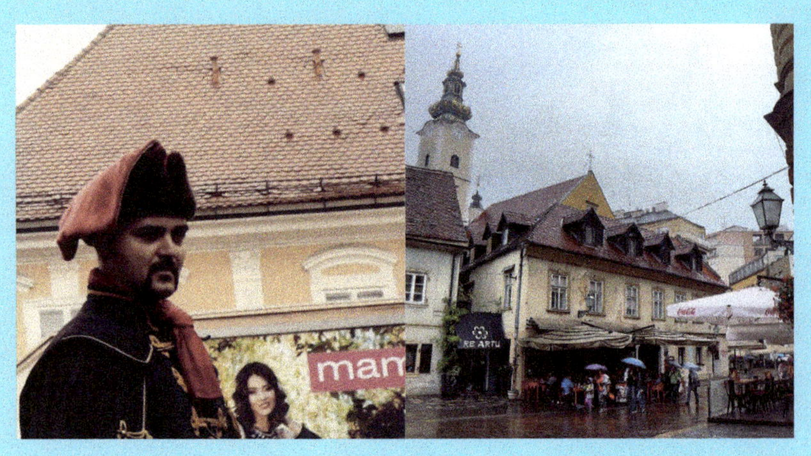
man
RE ARTU
Coca-Cola

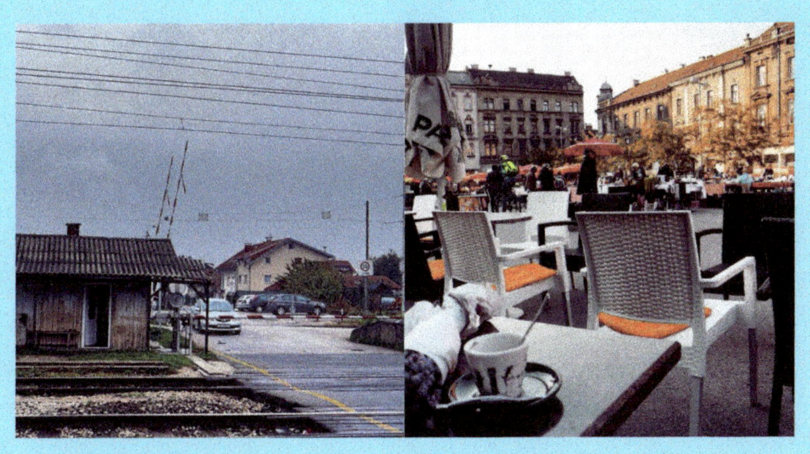